Illustrations by Isabel Muñoz.

Written by Jane Kent.

Designed by Nick Ackland.

White Star Kids® is a registered trademark property of White Star s.r.l.

© 2019 White Star s.r.l.
Piazzale Luigi Cadorna, 6
20123 Milan, Italy
www.whitestar.it

Produced by i am a bookworm.

ISBN 978-88-544-1364-1
 2 3 4 5 6   23 22 21 20 19

Printed in China

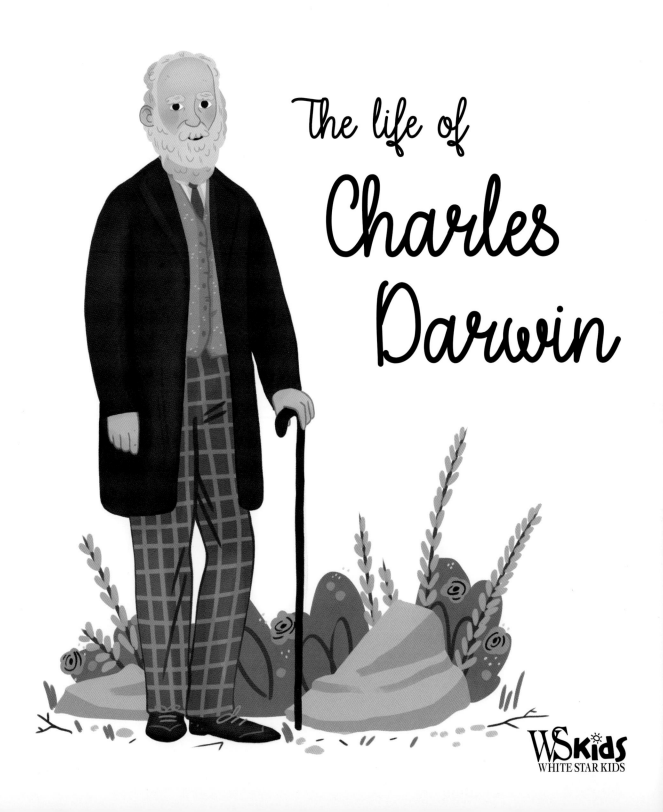

The life of Charles Darwin

I am Charles Darwin, the biologist who introduced
people to the theory of evolution and the process
of natural selection. At the time it was a highly
controversial idea, and one that many strongly
disagreed with.

Sail around the world with me, on a voyage filled
with adventure and an extraordinary new discovery
that would forever alter the way we look
at the world.

I was born on 12th February 1809, in the tiny English town of Shrewsbury. My father was a doctor called Robert and my mother, Susannah, was from the famous Wedgwood pottery family. They had six children - I was the second youngest - and raised us as Christians. When I was 8, my mother died and so my older sisters took care of me.

My grandfather, the renowned botanist Dr. Erasmus Darwin, was a freethinking physician. From 1794 to 1796 he wrote "Zoonomia", which put forward a radical and extremely contentious idea - that one species could 'transmute' into another.

I started at Edinburgh University in October 1825, when I was 16. My father wanted me to become a doctor, like him, and so I studied medicine. However, I wasn't the best student because I felt sick at the sight of blood.

I spent a lot of time discussing marine life with Robert Grant, a qualified doctor who had given up medicine in favor of marine biology, and I was elected a member of the Plinian Society 28th November 1826. It was a University club for students interested in natural history, where I met many radical freethinkers.

In October 1827 I enrolled at Christ's College, Cambridge, and began my studies there the following January. As medicine clearly wasn't the right path for me, my father suggested I study to become a clergyman instead.

My preferred subjects remained biology and natural history. Botany professor John Henslow became my mentor and I spent a lot of time out walking and collecting beetles. I finally graduated with a Bachelor of Arts degree in 1831.

Before I could find a job as a clergyman, I was given the opportunity of a lifetime. Henslow had recommended me for a naturalist's position aboard a brig called the HMS *Beagle*. It was to be a five year voyage around the world, to survey the coasts around the southern tip of South America.

Under Captain Robert FitzRoy, we set sail from Plymouth harbor on 27th December 1831, when I was 22. I was excited, although I did suffer with terrible seasickness.

I ensured I was well equipped before I set off, having sought advice
on preserving carcasses from experts at London Zoo.
We visited four continents in five years and I spent as much time on land
as possible, leaving the ship for extended periods to observing nature.

It was a unique opportunity to closely observe the principles of botany, geology and zoology. I did a lot of hands-on research and experimentation, in order to collect plant and fossil specimens and investigate the local geology.

In Brazil, I explored a rainforest. In Argentina, I discovered many fossils. On the island of Chiloé, I witnessed the volcanic eruption of Mount Osomo. Journal after journal was filled with meticulous field notes, which I then sent back home.

BRAZIL

ARGENTINA

CHILOÉ

When we left South America behind, we stopped 600 miles off the coast of Ecuador at the Galápagos Islands. Over five weeks, I spent time on four of the small volcanic islands - San Cristóbal, Floreana, Isabela and Santiago. I discovered that although each island had similar flora and fauna, they were perfectly adapted to their different environments.

We landed back in England on 2nd October 1836. My head was filled with all of the extraordinary things I had seen and experienced, so I immediately started to write up my findings.

The trip had had a monumental effect on me. My view of natural history had been altered and the seeds of a revolutionary new theory began to grow.

Having seen that animals most suited to their environment survived longer and had more young while those that failed to adapt and reproduce died off, I now believed that evolution occurred by a process that I called "natural selection". It was an idea I kept to myself for many years.

I was made a Fellow of the Geological Society in January 1837, presenting four papers on some of my findings aboard the *Beagle* and becoming secretary in 1838. That same year, on the 11th November, I proposed to Emma Wedgwood. Happily she accepted, and we married on 29th January 1839. We went onto have ten children, six boys and four girls.

At the time of my marriage, I was still struggling to go public with my new theory, because it went against my Christian beliefs and because of how my grandfather had been treated when he voiced his transmutation idea. So I shut my notebooks and instead published my travel diary, "Journal of Researches into the Geology and Natural History of the Various Countries Visited by H.M.S. *Beagle*", in 1839.

My belief in Christianity was shattered when my eldest daughter, Anne, died in 1851 at the age of 10. I never truly recovered from the loss and often became sick myself, suffering long periods of nausea throughout the rest of my life. The cause of my illness has never been confirmed. Some say I contracted a tropical disease on my travels, while others believe it was all in my head and that stressful events triggered it.

While still working on and expanding my theory, I published several books on coral reefs and South American geology. These works secured my reputation as a geologist and in 1853 I won the Royal Society's Royal Medal for my detailed study of barnacles. The following year, I was elected to the Royal Society's Philosophical Club.

By June 1858 I had written many thousands of words on evolution and natural selection, but they had been read by no one other than myself. I was given the push I needed to go public with my theory when I received a letter from Alfred Russel Wallace.

He had long been an admirer of mine, and my voyage on the *Beagle* had inspired him to go traveling himself. He then came up with his own theory of natural selection and had written to ask my advice on publishing it. If I didn't act quickly, Wallace would be credited with my ideas.

Wallace was abroad and could not be contacted, so I alone had to decide how to proceed. I wanted to ensure that I got credit for my ideas, while also acknowledging Wallace. So on 1st July 1858, my theory was publically revealed at a meeting of the Linnean Society, Britain's leading group on Natural History.

I had to miss the meeting because my youngest son, Charles, had died of scarlet fever aged just 18 months. So instead my friends Charles Lyell and Joseph Hooker read out a letter that I had prepared. They also presented extracts from both mine and Wallace's papers, which Wallace later agreed had been fair.

I then wrote and published a detailed explanation of my theory in November 1859. The book was called "On the Origin of Species by Means of Natural Selection". One key finding I hinted at was that human beings were descended from apes.

I dreaded losing my reputation, as my grandfather had, and although many people were shocked by my ideas, many others were willing to listen to me. My theory of evolution and the process of natural selection later became known as "Darwinism" and my book is now considered one of the most important ever written, going into multiple editions and selling worldwide.

After the publication of my book, any debate about evolution drew huge crowds. I was reluctant to attend, even to defend my ideas. However, a young biologist called Thomas Huxley was not afraid to take up what many viewed as the fight between science and God.

At a meeting of the British Association for the Advancement of Science in 1860, Huxley pitched my idea of evolution against Bishop Samuel Wilberforce's Biblical account of creation. With both sides claiming to be right, it was a clash that would go down in history.

On 30th November 1864, I was awarded the Copley Medal by the Royal Society. It was the oldest and most prestigious award, given annually for outstanding achievements in scientific research. By this time I was falling ill for longer and longer periods. Eventually my heart failed and I died at my family home on 19th April 1882.

I was buried at Westminster Abbey and my funeral was attended by many key figures in science. Five years after my passing, in 1887, the autobiography that I had begun writing in 1876 for the amusement of my grandchildren was published. And the following century, DNA studies would finally provide scientific evidence for my theory of evolution.

I hope my story inspires you to have faith in your own ideas and be brave enough to express them. Don't be afraid to challenge conventions, because that's how new ground is broken and important changes are made. There will always be people who disagree with you and others who support you, but the key thing is to have courage and believe in yourself.

Darwin was born on 12th February in Shrewsbury, England.

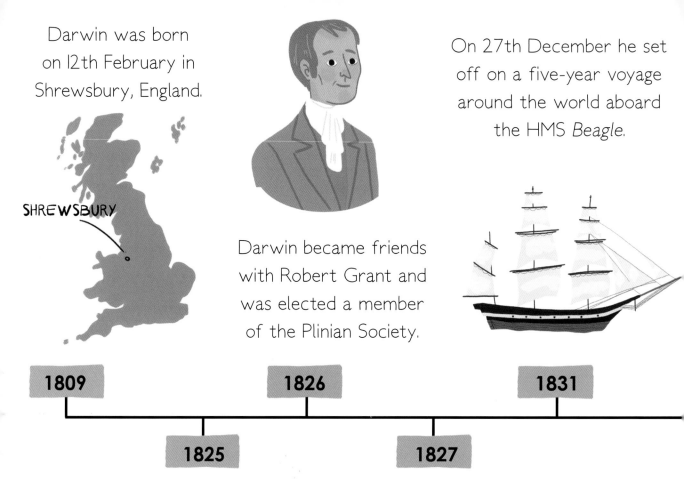

SHREWSBURY

On 27th December he set off on a five-year voyage around the world aboard the HMS *Beagle*.

Darwin became friends with Robert Grant and was elected a member of the Plinian Society.

1809   **1826**   **1831**

1825   **1827**

He started studying medicine at Edinburgh University, but was more interested in natural history.

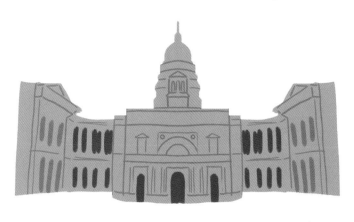

Darwin enrolled at Christ's College, Cambridge, to become a clergyman. Botany professor John Henslow became his mentor.

Darwin was made a Fellow of the Geological Society.

Darwin's travel diary, "Journal of Researches into the Geology and Natural History of the Various Countries Visited by H.M.S. *Beagle*", was published.

1837

1839

1836

1838

1842

Darwin arrived back in England on 2nd October. He immediately began writing up his findings.

He became secretary of the Geological Society and proposed to Emma Wedgwood.

The Darwin family moved to the village of Downe in Kent.

KENT

Darwin's eldest daughter, Anne, died and his Christian faith was shaken.

Darwin received a letter from Alfred Russel Wallace, prompting him to finally go public with his secret theory of natural selection. Charles passed away from scarlet fever.

Darwin was elected to the Royal Society's Philosophical Club and became a Fellow of the Linnean Society.

1851

1854

1858

1853

1856

Charles, Darwin's youngest son, was born.

His study of barnacles won Darwin the Royal Society's Royal Medal.

Thomas Huxley defended Darwin's theory in a debate with Bishop Samuel Wilberforce.

He passed away at home on 19th April and was buried at Westminster Abbey.

1860

1882

1859

1864

1887

Darwin was awarded the Copley Medal by the Royal Society.

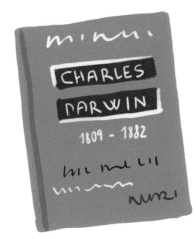

His book, "On the Origin of Species by Means of Natural Selection", was published.

Darwin's autobiography was published.

QUESTIONS

Q1. Who was Darwin's mentor at Cambridge?

Q2. What was the name of the brig that Darwin voyaged around the world aboard?

Q3. Which four Galapágos Islands did Darwin spend time on?

Q4. On what date did Darwin arrive back in England?

Q5. Which society was Darwin made a fellow of in 1837, and secretary the following year?

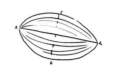

Q6. The study of what won Darwin
the Royal Society's Royal Medal in 1853?

_____

Q7. A letter from whom finally made Darwin
go public with his theory?

DARWI
JOURN

_____

Q8. What was the title of Darwin's
most famous book?

_____

Q9. Who did Thomas Huxley defend Darwin's theory against?

_____

Q10. Where is Darwin buried?

_____

ANSWERS

A1. John Henslow.

A2. The HMS *Beagle*.

A3. San Cristóbal, Floreana, Isabela and Santiago.

A4. 2nd October 1836.

A5. The Geological Society.

A5. Barnacles.

A7. Alfred Russel Wallace.

A8. "On the Origin of Species by Means of Natural Selection".

A9. Bishop Samuel Wilberforce.

A10. Westminster Abbey.

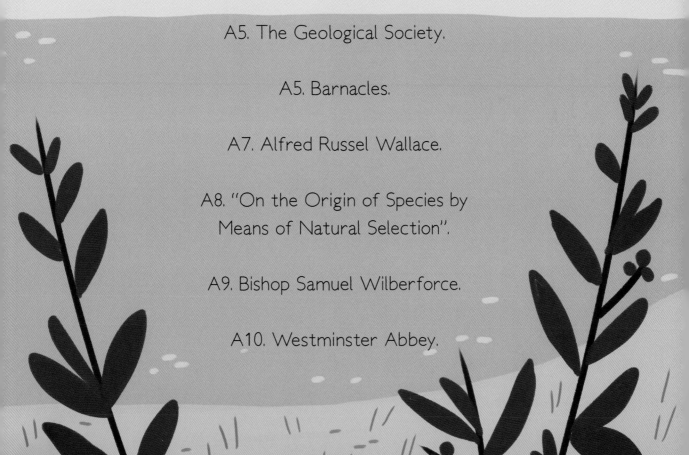